A P O L L O   I N   T H E   S N O W

Aleksandr Kushner

A P O L L O   I N

T H E   S N O W

Selected Poems

TRANSLATED BY PAUL GRAVES

AND CAROL UELAND

WITH AN INTRODUCTION BY

JOSEPH BRODSKY

Farrar, Straus and Giroux

NEW YORK

Library of Congress Cataloging-in-Publication Data
Kushner, Aleksandr.
Apollo in the snow : selected poems / Aleksandr Kushner ;
translated by Paul Graves and Carol Ueland ; with an introduction by
Joseph Brodsky.
Translated from the Russian.
1. Kushner, Aleksandr—Translations, English.   I. Graves, Paul.
II. Ueland, Carol. III. Brodsky, Joseph, 1940–   . IV. Title.
PG3482.8.U73A88   1991   891.71'44—dc20   90-46116

Some of these poems first appeared, in somewhat different form,
in *The American Poetry Review*, *Confrontation*, *The New York Review of
Books*, *Nimrod*, *Parnassus*, and *Partisan Review*.

Contents

1 9 8 0 – 1 9 8 7

Introduction

Time spent on an introduction is time stolen from reading, so I will be brief. Brevity, after all, is an attractive quality in any human utterance: when it comes to poetry, it is the mother of lyricism. Or, quite possibly, it is the other way around: lyricism is the mother of brevity. Which of these two propositions is correct remains for you to discover, for the poet before you is not an epic poet but a lyrical one.

I don't want to try to establish this or that mood. Nor is it my present intention to praise or to analyze the work of Aleksandr Kushner. Poems speak for themselves: for me to play the salesman, praising this poet's merchandise to you, the innocent customers—both of these roles are equally inappropriate. In these pages, you will find yourselves in a tête-à-tête with poetry in its pure form, the purest available to the Russian language—and prose has no business here. Yet I do consider it my duty to warn you that an encounter with poetry in its pure form is pregnant with far-reaching consequences, that this volume is not where it will all end for you. Aleksandr Kushner is one of the best Russian lyric poets of the twentieth century, and his name is destined to rank with those close to the heart of everyone whose mother tongue is Russian. This name is destined to outlive most of us and our children and grandchildren, as well as its bearer himself. I am saying this, not out of an abundance of personal sentiment and not as a fellow penman, but as a reader. To me, simply as a reader, it is all the more evident—if only because the twentieth century is running to its close; and even if something new springs out of the entrails of Russian literature, somebody very remarkable and perhaps even not inferior in talent to Aleksandr Kushner, this individual will have at his disposal but ten years. And in ten years, even possessing the most extraordinary gifts, nobody would be able to accomplish what has been accomplished by Kushner in the course of over three decades.

Thirty years in poetry is a lot of time. It's more than the entire creative career of Khlebnikov or Mayakovsky; it approximately equals that of Mandelstam; it spans almost the entire life of Pushkin. But we do not see our own contemporaries; because they are our contemporaries, we don't regard them in the categories of time. We regard them as our equals, don't acknowledge to ourselves the distance covered by them, don't subject them to retrospection.

In the course of these thirty years, Kushner covered an extraordinary distance, although his life is not rich in spectacular events and doesn't conform to our image of the poetic biography. (We are, I must say, almost corrupted by poetic biographies, with their predominantly tragic denomination—in this century especially.) A biography, even one saturated with momentous events, has a very remote relation to literature. Did that sort of dependency between fate and art indeed exist, the literature of the twentieth century, in Russia in any case, would present an entirely different picture. It's possible to spend twenty years in a prison camp, or to survive Hiroshima, and produce not a line. And it's possible, possessing no experience but a fleeting infatuation, to produce "the wondrous moment of our meeting."* Art differs from life precisely in that it takes no lessons from it, having very little to learn from a teacher so redundant. Art has its own past, its own present, its own future, its own logic and dynamic. And the biography of a poet is the biography—nay, the entire history!—of art: the biography of his material. More exactly, the biography of a poet lies in what he does with the inherited material; it is in his choice of means, in his meters and rhymes, in his stanzas, periods, and commas, in his diction—in what he picks out from this inherited material. In these thirty-odd years,

* From the opening lines of the famous poem by Aleksandr Pushkin.

Aleksandr Kushner has produced eleven books of poetry. For all their thematic diversity, their stylistic unity—the unity of Kushner's poetics—is phenomenal. If there is any kinship between poetry and life, it is in that, for both, the choice of means is of more consequence than the end. I am not discovering America, or even Russia, when I say that poetics itself is the content.

Any discourse on Kushner's poetic genealogy seems to me quite pointless. For a poet of this stature, there is no reason to adorn his dwelling with portraits of Pushkin, Fet, Annensky, or Kuzmin. But perhaps something could be done with the anteroom: Kushner's poetics is, of course, a combination of the Harmonious School and Acmeism. In our time, defiled as it is by poorly understood modernism, the choice of these means does not only testify to the spiritual integrity of the chooser. It indicates in the first place the organic character of these means for Russian poetry, their versatility, their viability. I would even venture to say that it is not Kushner who chose these means but the means that chose Kushner, in order to demonstrate, in the thickening chaos, the inclination of the language toward clarity, the tendency of the conscience to sobriety, of vision to lucidity, of the ear to precision—in other words, in order to demonstrate the durability of the species, the endurance of the very means themselves.

Kushner's poems are remarkable for their tonal reserve, their absence of hysteria, their sharp horizons, and their nervous gestures; he is rather dry where somebody else would boil, ironic where another would despair. Kushner's poetics, to put it differently, is the poetics of stoicism, and this stoicism is all the more convincing—and, I would add, infectious—because it is not the result of a rational choice, but in essence is a kind of exhalation, a consequence of extremely intense spiritual tension. In a poem, the testimony to spiritual tension is the intonation; or more accurately, intonation in a poem—and not in a poem only—stands for the motion of the soul. The mechanism of every Kushner poem is precisely the intonation, which subordinates the content, imagery, and—first of all—the meter. This mechanism, or, more exactly, this engine, runs neither on steam nor on turbine, but rather on internal combustion, which is perhaps the most apt definition of the form of the soul's existence, and perhaps what imparts to this engine characteristics of a *perpetuum mobile*.

The eleven books of poetry by Kushner that were published where they were published in the course of thirty years testify, in my view, not so much to the durability of this engine as to the inevitability of its existence—greater than that or any other political system, greater even than the very flesh in which it is housed. No system invented or manufactured this mechanism, and it is not for them to destroy it either. Poetry is essentially the soul's search for its release in language, and the work of Aleksandr Kushner is a case where the soul has obtained that release.

Joseph Brodsky
November 1988

1960–1974

The Decanter

Wonder of wonders! Water's limpid sphere
is kept from falling by a glass decanter.
Where does it come from? How did it appear
in this huge institution? As I stand here
transfixed beside the table, wondering which
gray, predawn park we had till now forgotten,
I'm happy knowing water's shape can switch,
always submissive to the form it's caught in.
And the decanter, out of emptiness,
floats like the ghost of an ice floe that melted
or like the answer to a dreamed request
by the unlucky dead whom thirst has wilted.

Having picked up a glass, should I now start
to take a sip, and feel how I can't stop its
arresting chill from spreading to the heart
unbearable compassion for all objects?
When I've talked with a girl from down the hall,
I'll sigh; you'd think she caused it, but it's not her.
No; separated by an unseen wall,
they're looking at each other: air and water.

It's longer, harder saying our goodbyes.
In France
how far apart are they in parting?
In Germany
what distance is worth remarking?
To get to Sakhalin it takes ten days.
Our loves are longer and more trying, too.
The summers here are harsher and much briefer.
Nights of desolation sever lovers;
in snowstorms, thousands of small lights slog through.
Between our lovers there spring up such squabbles,
such elevations and depressions . . .

                         The time
for late-night talks is, to us, invaluable,
as is the hot breath of a telegram.
The breath of our steam engines, too, is noisy,
breaking into cities at the crack of dawn.
Our mailbox latches opening and closing
click even at night, and all day long.
Go ahead and read about their foreign love,
about their holiday-like Western passions;
but when you hand the girl your ticket stub,
her greeting as she checks it against your baggage
recalls, remarkably, your wife's voice, and
you now must take a drink from that cup also.
You see, then, how our feelings can be altered
by the mere geography of the land.

God of family complaisance,
peaceful scenes, festivities,
you're like the greenhouse watchman, ancient
and kind amid the deities.

You have charged me with a baby,
you have given me my wife,
handed me a chair and table,
my towel, and the hush of night.

But the mastery and abundance
marking Dutch pictorial style
doesn't give you peace, and hinders
you in drawing what you will.

Since we know to value money,
you have drawn us at our work;
and yet you regard more fondly
frolic scenes and flower bursts.

In my hand you place a wineglass,
toss some wildfowl on the board,
and seat us in a circle, finding
still you can't perceive our core.

Though we'll take our proper places,
we won't satisfy you there:
we'll exchange our human glances
and stroke our little boy's fair hair.

No, not one face, but two: the world
has two wings also, and two meanings.
Two fathers, not just one, occur
in Shakespeare, crying out for vengeance.

When Hamlet sees Laertes' pain,
his binoculars are backwards;
but if this boy's an insect, then
why is the insect's face tear-spattered?

The wrinkles at their mouths are the same;
the same domestic problems needle
both, caught in such a narrow frame
they can't even turn around completely.

You touched a shoulder and you stopped
the turning at a half-turn, matching
the turning of a key in a lock
that pushes someone into action.

Hastily one of you walks out;
one of you hides his hand in a hurry.
Then you look back, crying, distraught,
to see someone else weeping near you.

By leaving, you opted for space.
But time would have been as effective.
Both remedies bring you the ease
of ultimately just forgetting.
And even if you hadn't left,
the end wouldn't be any different.
You watch mist spread over the steppe
and shadows fly into the distance,
then, all of a sudden, come to:
where are you? Dzhankoi? —Doesn't matter.
See, there's not one Lethe but two;
and it's the same, drinking from either.

The Adoration of the Magi

Off one of Moscow's smaller streets
that a snowstorm had covered,
we saw the cradle's tiny sheets;
like magi we leaned over.

And something gleamed, as if the child
were swathed in a faint halo;
bottles and plates of food were piled
in offering on the table.

In the half-dark we looked around
and then once more bent forward,
dreaming a cow and calf lay down
and eyed us from the corner.

—A scene that Hugo van der Goes
would draw: a beaded necklace
for the housewife; the magi muse
while through the door light trickles.

And we were filled with such a sense
of peace that, as we shared it,
we couldn't fear the violence
or threats of any Herod.

The world's whole horror, from day one
to now, stood at a distance;
as if under a spell it hung
and yielded for an instant.

And the Volkhonka then became
as aged as the Bible,
while light snow on the windowpane
welcomed a child's arrival.

It gathered us from where we live;
through street and park we stumbled,
following, as we always have,
a miracle so simple.

No woman that I'd met before
threw money in the fire, or ever
shuddered in sudden bouts of fever,
sheet-white, while standing at the door.
Nor, in cold concert halls or parks
—thank God—had one, somewhat excited,
just as her legs were warming slightly,
pulled a revolver from her purse.

Ridiculous! And still I wouldn't know
the fatal shadows people talk of
if those wild little shoes had walked off
instead of bringing her hello.
Cheap perfume's reek pervades the rooms;
nothing's discreet or wise about her:
she blots her teary cheeks with powder
and raves about atrocious poems.

Hoffmann

Wait a minute, there's something I'd like to ask:
Did Hoffmann find having three names an easy task?
He had to bear three people's grief and tiredness, alias
Ernst and Theodor and Amadeus.
Ernst is just a cog, the legal-office sort
who's busy scribbling page after page in court.
He doesn't draw, he doesn't make things up or sing;
he just creaks along in the bureaucracy's machine.

He creaks and sweats, and tries to shorten convicts' terms.
Theodor is so much luckier than Ernst.
His shoulder hurts when he gets home, but he ignores it,
he lights a candle and spends the whole night writing stories.
He's writing stories, but he's increasingly disheartened;
then Amadeus knocks at Theodor's apartment.
The unexpected and beloved visitor,
like Mozart, throws up his hands and waves them in the air.

On the Friedrichstrasse, Hoffmann has his coffee.
"Down the Friedrichstrasse," Ernst says very softly.
"No, no; go right instead," pleads Theodor. A third
voice tells them both, "Turn left into that yard."
And in the yard an oh-so-tentative flute suggests
a child whose finger points him through the alphabet.
"But even so," sighs Amadeus, "it excels
in sweetness both judicial codes and tales."

Here I am—my chair is wobbly—
sitting in a tiny room,
drinking up some Georgian bubbly
that our guests left unconsumed.

We're unhappy—what's the reason?
No one loves us—who's so mean?
Down my back a sharp sensation
of snow beyond the curtained pane.

Winter holidays are coming:
fir trees, streamers, cotton wool.
Snow and sparkling wine's aroma
grow every year more beautiful.

So with love: the repetitions
don't get dull, they simply bring
more of knowledge, more of patience,
more unimaginable things.

It struck me that two darks,
a first one and a last,
around our lives stand guard
and shadow every face.

But don't compare the thick
dark, native to the grave,
with that more neighborlike
antecedent shade.

How lightly I can look
at snapshots of past years:
"The armchair," I'll remark,
"but me? I'm not yet there."

With horror, though, I glance
beyond the blackest bound,
to where an armchair stands
in which I once sat down.

It's the way things are arranged
on the table's expanse,
the way that light is splayed
through the blue ice of glass . . .

Put poppies, tulips here; set out
the goblet in its place.
So, are you happy? No. And now?
Not quite. And now? Oh yes!

The envelope looks so peculiar,
so odd, perhaps the sender made it
himself; the nebulous postmark's older
than a week—in fact, it looks quite aged.
The stamp, as well, is strange and empty,
the washed-out shape of some backcountry:
no Uruguayan president or
view of the Thames—just stunted shrubbery.

The characters are squeezed together
too close: the hand is clearly cryptic.
Below, as you might have gathered,
no return address is written.
I open the edge, tearing it gently,
and on the heavy sheet of paper
with difficulty parse a sentence,
the Russian words completely haywire.

"We've huddled closely in a circle;
this sign of our concern gives witness
to you of our own universal,
faded, weakening existence.
And when at night"—but this is delirious!—
"the wind is battling the dark garden,
we won't speak all our names, but hear us:
we're right beside you—ssh, don't be startled.

"Don't sleep, though; be more scrutinizing,
so each of us can be distinguished."

I skip some undecipherable writing
and come abruptly to the finish:
"Farewell! Our ink is getting fainter,
our mails can hardly be relied on,
and the leaves have gotten so much rain here
that we can't take a step in the garden."

Our tastes mark us as unromantic.
We'll be consoled through all our days
by hair teased into shape, and sandy;
a feminine and comely face,
its features softened just a little,
and a slight upturn to the nose.
Where's Fate, with killing eyes that glitter?
Such frenzy isn't even close.

The brows weren't adequately penciled
and the eye shadow was too light.
One lip closed on its mate and pressed it
to keep the tears shut up inside.
Don't cry: they all will pass, the empty
old dreams—and all of life will dart.
Oh, the means you use against me
—how simple! Yet you break my heart.

In the cold of Petropavlovsk, Peter dreams
        about fortress bulwarks;
while the lips of Leningrad's beauties freeze
        to a bluer color.

A woman's cruel silhouette, a high brow that gray
        thistly hoarfrost fringes . . .
Thus, it follows that love won't anticipate joy,
        that it pierces like splinters.

No mouth's raspberry tint will grant me a smile.
        Expect nothing so tender
—instead, something more like a sneer, and (I can't lie)
        a recognition of error.

So much water already in the blackened Neva,
        and it keeps on swelling.
There is nothing on earth to outweigh this sigh
        through the iron-boughed railing.

What's the subject? An article that just appeared
        in a philosophy journal,
about archetype, myth, our own lives, and our
        powers of discernment.

Everything's repetition: aspirations and dreams,
        and the snarling of ogres.
But for me, only the element of novelty seems
        worthwhile or engrossing.

The snow twists, as if dreamily knitting a scarf;
    everywhere it flickers,
hoping to lead our conversation's thread off
    toward sewing and knitting.

The insane horseback idol stands over the abyss,
    frozen, eerily coupled
in the mind with a silvery truck hauling gas
    and a synthetic sable.

O fame, you have passed us by like the rain, vanished
outright like a film from the West we never managed
to see, like the last streetcar turned into the yard.
We don't need you now, you're not worth it. *Au revoir!*

Your chariot's broken down out on the highway,
the last bird has followed the southerly flyway,
the last motorboat is gone from the Neva.
I walked to the Moika—no, winter's not far.

The hunger for fame no longer torments us;
we're caught up in other ideas, new conventions;
my lover sleeps, and in the autumn night's hush
don't let any rumors of me wake her up.

Mist blankets the city; light snow starts to settle.
A poster's frozen with a piano recital.
The door spring pulls shut with a hollow whack.
My temples still throb for the last rhyme to click.

We'll say farewell with half-words, tersely and dryly.
The music will slowly peter out into silence,
like water that spills from the ears after a swim,
a lukewarm, diminutive, ticklish stream.

Someone's crying all night.
Just behind the wall someone's crying.
    If I could, I would try
to help, but the aggrieved won't invite me.

    It's stopped. No, there it is.
"Go to sleep," you say. "Sleep; you imagined . . ."
    I need rest, I need rest.
In the dark, though, my heart's contracted.

    People crying these days?
Where'd you hear any crying, I wonder.
    No age kept dryer eyes
than ours, raised under a tearless banner.

    Maybe children—but they,
hearing, "Shame on you!," will fall silent.
    So in darkness we lie;
only the watch on the table's unquiet.

    Someone's crying nearby.
"Sleep," you tell me again; "I don't hear it."
    If I asked, your reply
would give rain on the roof as your theory.

    It's stopped. Now it starts up,
as if there's still more, deeper grief, hiding.
    But I'm falling asleep.
"Wake up! Listen!" you say. "Someone's crying."

In a Café

To Joseph Brodsky

Here, in an overcrowded and deafening café,
I've been duped with warm wine, overlooked as if I
were a price's last-column figure.
My companion, sick of his unsavory meal,
admires the nickel-silver ring bearing a seal
that he's got on his littlest, hairy finger.

The sky, darkening toward dusk, is suspended outside
like damp linen absorbing a spill. The sun's light
glances in just to touch my companion,
and the signet ring burns with a samovar's blaze.
"Hey, should we get some girls to come over?" he says;
then, with boredom: "There's nobody stunning."

He's immediately plunged back in the general murk,
keeping silent because I've ignored his remark.
He's cross: why don't we get the check settled?
But the waiter's not hurrying over to us;
he's just straightening his tie in front of the glass.
I stare at the ring—I can't help it.

It works magic! Its owner, though, doesn't know that.
Just a turn on his finger beneath the dull flat
of the table, and behold: the blue ocean
and a coral reef that boiled up out of Monet,
from a canvas that was briefly here on display,
looking violet-white and imposing.

One more turn, and here's Yalta in winter, where the black,
dirty rim of a coal ship approaches the dock,
like black crepe in a funeral procession.
A ray flickers and wells up again, like a spring.
Was it over the counter that he bought this ring,
or at work in the hard-goods sector?

But I gasp at the third time the signet ring turns.
It's too frightening to speak of; all possible words
miss the point or look suddenly diminished:
Will it ever put this red-haired friend at our door?
Will it sweep this strange fellow away from us—or
return him his youth to begin with?

At the window I watch the nocturnal clouds pass,
having pushed back the spartan curtain.
I've been happy, and fearful of death. Now I'm less
afraid—not unafraid, but less urgent:

since to die means to stir aloud in the wind
with the maples, bowed under together.
Since to die means to come to the court of a king,
of a Richard, or maybe an Arthur.

Since to die is to crack a tough nut, opening up
all the reasons and motives once hidden.
Since to die is to become the contemporary of
everyone, except the still living.

Remembering Love

I am forbidden to look back.
Not because her precious shade is thus surrendered
    but because, hidden along my path,
she actually draws nearer, so that I turn pensive
    and miserable again, when I already thought
I was cured, a survivor.
    And like lung tissue, pieces of the soul are soft:
it's not yet calcified all over.

There is design in agony, design in loss,
    as in the grapevines' Phylloxera.
The soul is stricken by a brilliant, far-off,
    unattainable chimera.
No, don't look back! but let the snow and rain wash out
    every last blemish.
I was in torment—for whom? I was in mourning—for what?
    I don't look back, so I don't comprehend it.

My flimsy paperback explains the rescue attempt
    as a mechanism of displacement.
No, don't look back! The feverish soul, though, won't accept:
    "Just once! Only in passing!"
Shouldn't I look? It is a treacherous path.
    Imagine I stumbled. For didn't
Orpheus himself, who kept repeating, "Don't look back,"
    look back because it was forbidden?

1975 – 1979

Apollo in the Snow

A colonnade, with Apollo, in snow.
A white cap's fitted over his wreath;
and while yellowish titmice hold
on to him, snowdrifts shackle his feet.
Dazzled, standing with eyes cruelly stung
by the lashings of silvery dust,
he looks mottled where moisture has sunk
into crevices and icy lumps.

The immobility of frozen boughs
was unimaginable in the hilly climes,
hemmed by olives and sea-deep blues,
of his Mediterranean twins;
but here, shielded by empty gray nests,
where the snow looks like plaster or chalk,
is his most northerly, far-flung post
—and his influence's boundary mark.

With a huge country stretching beyond,
on these cloistered shores laced in with ice
the lyre's moans, stilled by frostbite, grow faint
and are snuffed out by snow, day and night;
so it seems these sounds have no use,
neither now nor for many years hence
—but perhaps the more painful for us,
and for him, to sing, the sweeter it gets.

The soul gleams in the white spikes of a wreath;
ice and twilight have lodged in its cracks.

This frost-breathing stone deity bequeaths
us the victory palm for our task.
This palm, probably twisted from fir,
has been dusted all over with rime.
Here is courage. And here snowstorms swirl.
Here, enveloped in shivers, are these lines.

Folded Wings

Now the butterfly's color
will blend into the bark's when its wings quickly fold.
    Could our peering uncover
        a butterfly? No.

Woe unto us, woe and sorrow!
—Matched in every detail: not a crack, not a stitch.
    As, in ancient Greek chorus,
        strophe, antistrophe latch.

See how rich we were once; now it's all been squandered.
We had hopes of retrieving the splendor—too late, as it seems.
Where's your palace? In grief, blinded, stumbling, you wander,
        Oedipus, the King.

Now that joy's wings have folded,
it peers out from its verso, its wretched, dispirited side.
    What the soul had held closest
has become a continuous trial.

    And your handwriting changes.
    In the search for a line you bend
and retrieve nothing but a dead leaf, shrunken, dingy,
        though you'd thought you felt wings flutter under your hand.

    And time turns into twilight.
Where's the velvety fabric, the canvas, pattern and ground?
    Life is altered, benighted;
the design, lost in mist, is almost too indistinct to be found.

What varieties of flashy butterflies once surfaced, enticing
us with Paris in violet hues or with warm tropic air!
        My heart stopped in excitement,
till a voice whispered, "You shouldn't be looking there!"

        No, but look more intently,
        on all sides, before turning to plunge
back to yourself. Even love might be here, only folded; when it
finds a perch it stays, loving silently, placing wing over wing.

And perhaps even good, if it's genuine, is surreptitious,
is accomplished in secret, is totally dark,
        satisfies no suspicion
as to how it's been done, doesn't show you a chink or a crack.

Perhaps, too, it's our fault the butterfly folded its brilliant,
fiery wings: maybe we simply walked up too close.
We'll part; it will take wing and revive like Princess Brambilla
        from the harlequin dust.

The Bush

The jasmine bush turns into an evangelist,
grown white at twilight, redolent of showers;
along mosquito-ringing lanes, it manages
to tell no less than Matthew at such hours.

How damp and white, what shining clustered heaviness,
and how the wilding petals scatter, shaken!
You're deaf and blind if you require more evidence
for the miraculous than their persuasion.

You're deaf and blind and look for someone suitable
to blame; but you yourself are the offender.
The bush, though, brushes you as you stare stupidly
in rage—and there your speech and sight are mended.

September picks up a wide broom and it sweeps
out beetles, small spiders in their see-through webs,
frayed butterfly rags, wasp husks' shriveled remains,
and broken-off stems of smashed dragonfly wings;
bugs' circular lenses—like eyeglasses or
binoculars—buttresses, scales, pollen down,
antennae, claws, pincers, maxillae that were
becoming once; frills from which life has flown.

September picks up a wide broom and it whisks
out chitinous residue and lacy shifts,
as if the conservatory's *maître de ballet*
woke suddenly, whooshing his dancers away.
September's wide broom sweeps out past the steps,
past fields, past the brook, and still farther, to plunge
in darkness the cuffs, raincoats, fastenings, hopes
of happiness, fans, batiste, bits of old fringe.

Goodbye, then, my joy, till the graveyard of wasps,
the scrap heap of beetles, the churchyard of flies,
the kingdom of Pluto, dry tears—till we've crossed
to the withering blooms of Elysian bliss.

Look: bronze. This statue was poured in obedience to
a model of wax, which itself was made up from a plaster-
cast prototype, marbly white, ancient Roman, on view
from an excavated Tivolian villa where, two
millennia, it lay under cover of earth, sleeping fast and
perhaps dreaming of its Hellenic original, which
has never reached us. We have taken it, copy from copy,
in a metamorphic progression. Bronze idol, in your
dull metal, all green! Recollecting the past leaves me tired;
and you? . . . still remembering another age, another body?

You still recall everything; I, in recalling, grow tired:
there's childhood, streetcars on Bolshoi Prospekt,

                                               the war's legless,
and how in the announcer's voice something like metal was heard.
I know who I was; as to who I became—well, that's clear,
too clear: all my joys, all my griefs, shame, love, and offenses.
I'd like to forget some of that, since I'm not the same one
now, anyway, the one to whom I bear no more relation.
Oh, how many layers, how many ages I have put on!
And fate picks me up, scraping and planing me in its hand;
it melts down and molds me—it even bronzes me faintly.

We don't get to choose our century,
and we exit after entering.
Nothing on this earth is cruder
than to beg for time or blame
the hour. No marketplace maneuver
can achieve a birth's exchange.

Though all ages are the iron age,
lovely gardens steam and varnished
cloudlets sparkle. I, at five,
should have died of scarlet fever;
live, avoiding grief and evil
—see how long you can survive.

Looking forward to good fortune?
Hoping for a better portion
than the Terrible's grim reign?
Leprosy and plagues in Florence
aren't your dream? The hold's dark storage
doesn't suit your first-class aims?

Though all ages are the iron age,
lovely gardens steam and varnished
cloudlets sparkle. I embrace
my age and my fated ending.
Time is an ordeal, and envying
anyone is out of place.

I embrace it firmly, knowing
time is flesh instead of clothing.
Deep in us its seal is set,
as if fingerprints were signals
of an age's lines and wrinkles.
In our hands our time is read.

In the morning, drafts in the blinds and curtains
occupy themselves sculpting quick busts and live torsos.
How they rustle and clap! I love their exertions,
their world piled with Uranidae, bulged like Colossus.

First a knee—then a shoulder, imprisoned in linen,
pushes out; they knock and shove in hopes of escaping
from their jail of cloth, but they'll fail to get in and
see the room, too weak to rip the light, pleated draperies.

World of giants! Angered by their blinded condition,
they are doomed to swell all morning with blisters;
first they sag, then rise back to a kneeling position,
stuck to doorknobs or caught on the edges of pictures.

It's like Pergamum's altar, with air for a lining!
No one needs to climb to the quarry for marble.
They will battle all morning: now one, sent flying,
grabs another; they tumble. Remember this marvel.

The whole morning, while you're still in bed, feeling lethargic,
after night's healed the stings that left you embarrassed,
Titans, rounded and crowded like columns, still argue
in the curtains, and struggle—and finally perish.

Man with a Rose

This is the portrait of a man
holding a rose by its slender
and pliant stem between two fingers,
turning its underside toward himself,
both swaggering and fastidious,
like every man.

There's no doubt: he is a man.
Vienna's analyst would waste
his time in trying to put the rose
through his ordeal: fetishism,
perhaps? Repressed deviations?
No, there's no source for them to spring from.

And furthermore, the rose is speechless
and, tired from twirling in his hand,
forgets where its tormentor is,
or where the table, chair, bouquet . . .

Splendid mustache and a caftan:
the man who holds the half-dead rose
stares, wondering what to do with it.
To breathe in its most subtle fragrance
never enters his mind, of course;
to pluck it and present it to
a lady—that's a different matter.
So men always conduct themselves;
and so a man has to handle life
a little carelessly

and overlook its smothered beauty,
like this admirable officer
(this isn't the place to cast reproaches)
with his awkwardness and slight mistakes,
because, more than for life, he itches
for valor, honor, and the like.

As at every doorstep grow rowan and maple,
so also at ours rose Rastrelli and Rossi;
as children know fir trees from pines, we were able
to distinguish Empire from Baroque without pausing.

So what, if all those pseudo-classical classics
strike us as examples of some sort of bathos?
The toga, in dense smog and encircled by traffic,
wraps round the great general like a sheet in a bathhouse.

We take such conventions as this one for granted;
we're used to it, for one thing. And when we were children
and saw this droll oddity, grownups explained it
to us as we came here, our small hands in their big ones.

These folds that were mightily rendered in copper
and stuck to the body—that is, to his jacket—
arranged to appear irreproachably proper,
give children a faith in a world where they'll make it

to similar fame. And we have to confess it's
a beauty from every angle of vision,
especially when a stray leaf hangs, pirouetting
in air, and autumn, banner-like, stands in the distance.

The dust in a shaft of late sun turns the distance
to haze, and the nearby grove is fogged over.
The painter's so quiet that, changing positions,
he finds a mouse in his pocket, taking cover.

Alas, her small body is funny and wretched.
He frowns with distaste. He pulls her from his pocket
—and then hides a smile, because being respected
as God is nevertheless flattering, exotic.

And what if he, too, in his usual ratty,
paint-spattered gray jacket, exploiting his spryness,
poked into what promised to be an inviting
large pocket that offered the hope of some kindness?

Would whoever found him then jump up, uneasy?
and smother him? shelter him? free him undamaged?
for meekness, for looking both fragile and busy,
still true to the field in whose dust he would vanish?

Vyritsa

Autumn turns the river furious,
frightening in its headlong passage
of indigo and iron-colored gusts.
Algae are stripped and tossed
in the current like rags the wind tatters.

Leaves have fallen, and this settlement,
Vyritsa itself, has settled, revealing
everything: the green blinds have been
torn away. A thin
row of firs remains, and then a clearing.

It's too bad old Vasya can't escape
from his wife: the construction worker's
every attempt to shuffle or evade,
every figure of eight,
can be seen by the most distant observer.

To keep winter from breaking their whips,
dormant raspberry canes are tied together.
This is not the finest place there is;
Vyritsa's the pits,
in fact: utterly third-rate, no better.

They have gone—and left the armchair out
in the yard; this seasonal existence
is too dissipated. Were we so loud
when we lived here? Now
life's left Vyritsa and what persists is

just pathetic traces. Paradise
on earth is brief, puffed away by autumn.
Was it really all carefree and light,
really a gentle life?
You've come alive, but trouble's not forgotten.

And sometimes you dream over again
the same dream you had last year. It's curious,
as if dreams were stored and copied; then,
on a different print,
rewound, they return from the warehouse.

I myself arranged my life like this;
so I won't complain, since it's connected
with life in general. I take risks,
blow so that my breath nips
the water's heat, and enter a treacherous decade.

A small bush nods and struggles with the wind,
and the withered grass is swept by shivers.
I am not cast down.
There are bound to be some ripples in
the branch when there's commotion in the river.

There are poets who look through a lens,
who are always snapping their own portraits.
Running from the tripod, they take their stance
with a lowered glance,
as if ignoring insult, playing orphans.

Only poems surpass the fullness of prose.
If it's possible to turn up answers
to the questions, and yet refuse
to adopt a pose
or focus on oneself in clipped-off stanzas . . .

But no binoculars will aim at us.
It's impossible for me to imagine
anybody's life without that dusk.
My hands are ice.
It's okay here, though the shore is fragile.

Sometimes I'm drawn to this desolate shore.
As is known, its slope betrays a leaning
toward thought. So those in the parterre,
beyond the stage hysteria, bored
with it all, start leaving.

45

I loved. I'd wake, not recollecting myself;
but my lover's name would break memory's surface,
two syllables known as if always, as if
at night they became mine somehow by transference;
and, rising, I'd push the sheets off in a hurry.

Just thinking of her, of course, ended all rest;
so it didn't last long. And again the obsession.
I loved; and it seemed I couldn't get past
the doors without thrice entering into temptation:
of parting with self amid all I possessed.

And the old Norwegian, who taught the bad blood
of love to our grandmothers, would drop to the table,
reread once again, in my miserable mood,
more keenly than newer books: firs, fjords, a cave-in
of ice, and, from under his bangs, the author, gazing.

To tell you the truth, this world's simply too rich:
that nests are destroyed it considers as nothing;
the censuring glance we cast leaves it untouched;
written words burn, stars fall from their stations,
and into the garden at night hard frosts encroach.

I loved; and stood near the machinery, close
to the earthly and heavenly mainsprings—as later
wouldn't happen again. Not the knowledge of cause
but knowledge of whim; not in the entry, waiting,
but ticketed to the four-postered chambers.

I loved; and probably also was loved;
that is, was discarded, picked out, and tormented.
Heartrending, hysterical youth was too rough;
with age, I endure the whole thing much better.
Beasts seemed then like creatures to be envious of!

I loved; and still . . . no, I feel nothing like that,
no, not anymore; now that's all over and finished.
And only my dreams lag behind; they don't yet
realize I'm awake, they love the riddles intrinsic
in curtains and blinds, in all gathers and wrinkles.

I loved . . . oh, when was that? I've forgotten now, but
it's been a long time—not this life, not this era,
some other. How foreign that ardor has proved
to be: all that fire, and wet cheeks, and etcetera.
So what's all this fuss—that I loved? So I loved . . .

This country, huge, wintry, and blue,
looms like the cloud outside our window.
Despite our wine and talk, this view
is not effaced. Though we leaf through
a German sketchbook, though we wind on
through our languorous novel and bend
over our work, we cannot help it:
we leave the foreground to the land,
to fog and streetlights that have lent
the snow its look of being gilded.

. . . Just as those who expect a car,
a phone call, telegram, or letter
turn halfheartedly to start
discussing drama, debating
or praising an act or a line . . .
Isn't it something amazing
to be so captivated, yet mind
the door, ears cocked and waiting?

When it's thirteen below, the mind begins preparing
itself, dreaming the world will end.
The streetcar's frozen through, turned to a long ice carriage.
The frozen milk is foamy, blind, and crystalline.

We have no strength to warm ourselves at home, to usher
the blood-red mercury back up through our chilled veins.
All day in Russia
we're pricked beyond the pale; we hardly dare to glance . . .

And sure enough, an avalanche! Aren't they amusing,
warning us not to leave doors open to the frost!
The avalanche plunges in silver-shot confusion.
This world's so cold—though we haven't felt the worst.

And suddenly the way that stretched for ages shrivels:
we've come full circle; see how little time it took!
That passenger, ridiculous, endearing, shivers,
his back forever vanishing in homeless smoke.

His sleigh rug's buttoned now; there's no need to disturb him.
I can't call out to him through smoke and freezing mist.
For five days now, not knowing why, I have been working
through fragments of Sumerian and Akkadian myth.

First all the demons wail, and then burst into dances.
But who inspired their uncontrollable mass rage?
A god entreats some help; they knock him to his senses.
The tablet with the text is broken at that place.

49

We won't find any substitute for that clay tablet.
We'll mourn the scattered kingdoms and the shepherd-god.
The snowstorm whips the foam. It's cold here on our planet.
And lines that once have perished cannot be recaught.

On this, the near side of the mystery line, a cloud
darkens to blue; the bushes bristle, fanning out.
On this side, my eye is irritated by an eyelash;
the table's filled with signs of my beloved work
on this side, this side, this . . . but there, beyond the mark,
there not a single button will roll through stillness.

But it will veer off, wobble, and decide to stop.
My hands have loved to turn things over and over; I've got
to unlearn that. It's time now for reeducation
by impenetrable darkness, dumbness, and divorce
—for like this button, I've begun to spin before
an undetected line with a shuddering, tiring motion.

Pan

With a lamb on his shoulders, the god
took in each hand two legs of the creature.
He, eternal, immortal, cannot
understand why the sheep suffers torture.

But the sheep's life nears its last stroke.
Perhaps he will just shear it, release it?
He bears it, like a child round his neck,
through his backwoods archaic region.

And the lamb cannot figure it out;
it hangs down from his shoulders, thinking
about why its waves haven't been cut
—after all, they, too, hang down in ringlets.

It's too bad: all these yeanlings and lambs
—their eyes widen and fill up with anguish.
But the victim himself, in our times,
we'll be told, comes to think his role standard.

How unencumbered and swift are the clouds!
Then a puff of smoke like wool or cotton.
And the victim would fall to a god's
hands, a grip that all four legs are caught in.

No better fate is given than to die in Rome.
I woke up with this phrase—like something out of Gogol.
Above a fountain's rainbow splashing on the stone
May's youthful skies learn how to blush without a struggle.

No better fate is given . . . Rome is springlike: all
its world is painted the unearthly hue of lilacs.
No better fate is given . . . shadows, however, fall,
death's shadows—but wait, on that I'm keeping silent.

The sun is swarthy, and circles of ash are found
smoldering under skies blue-eyed as flames' blue centers;
stone warriors' knees are pressed immobile to the ground;
like shadows under eyes lie epitaphs' reminders.

No better fate is given us than Rome . . . a man
who's on his way to God in Rome is one verst closer.
No better fate . . . or, maybe snow is better than . . .
no, better still is white snow flying on the road, or . . .

no, better this, cloud-closed and only one-third known,
whose features snowstorm, mist, and flurry blind and scatter.
No better fate is given than to die in Rome.
We'll die without you, though: we don't want any better.

Your exit's into frost, and the audience exits
onto a street where it's too cold for them to act,
where multitudes of cars never lower their headlights,
where snow lets up awhile, preparing to come back.
A stage-set look settles over the icy city;
what actors it has seen—we simply don't match up!
The snowy foam in parks receives another whipping,
and snow dust is puffed from a bridge's arching slope.

Well, dearest, then our work is just like anybody
else's work—and our love, of course, like any love.
The strain your voice betrays—I don't know where you got it;
don't contradict me now: calm down, enough's enough.
Maybe classicism, in its sunset glory,
is bound to thrust a tragic role on each of us,
with Terror entering our play of the ordinary,
so woman's laughter caves, like snow, into wet slush.

We meet a passerby ridiculously waving
his arms and talking to himself; his crazy eyes
never stop roving; he won't say what fear or craving
torments and drives him on through life, but madly cries:
". . . If someone climbed up there where the tragic mask is
and ripped it off the pediment—that mask's to blame—
and if we could wipe off the purple paint that plasters
night—with not the world as exit, but some other way . . ."

How stormily on the sarcophagus' white panels
life seethes! Here's passion, spring, and proud Hippolytus
striving with a dog and a horse too fast to handle,
out to spurn the letter from his stepmother's house.

We stood for a long time before the marble story.
Death has been surrounded on four sides by life
and clings to salty waves, to terraces and stairways,
to hunting and a love the stone hides from our sight.

There someone sleeps, bitterly—only the living
sleep sweetly. Slowly circling the scenes, we see death
and life as a dichotomous kernel, unriven—
the stone of death engraved with the life of this earth.

A crowd of stableboys are led by, looking lighthearted;
the waves are stretched out; the old nurse's back is bowed:
death embellishes life like a skillful carving.
Without death's presence, who could make the subject new?

As coal is used for cleaning a white horse,
as stove black's scrubbed with sand dredged from the river . . .
But now bad weather's banging at the doors;
the soul turns down the benefits in store.
How tell the soul it would be cleaner after?

On catching wind of grief and insults, it
always looks backwards to reiterate
the whole: that from delight, as well, soot issues,
and that a kiss, a painting, or the sight
of distant surf cries, too, beseeches . . .

It pleases me that Bakst, Nijinsky, and Benois
could find themselves in a page of Proust, occurring
among imaginary characters; the complex cloth
envelops one more stitch. They would be disconcerted
by the fame that earned them, while still alive, the right
to enter the intricacies of such a novel
—as if they heard their judgment handed down from right
and left, in the opinion of the grass and water.

Imagine: one sat fiddling with his cigarette
while holding volume four, thinking he'd stop reading,
when suddenly he thought he heard himself addressed
by the flowering hawthorns or some celestial being
out of a cloud. Let music play, the dancer rise
into a spinning torso, the painting never vanish;
how joyfully Parisian martins weave the sky!
Fate is most intricate and death presents no menace.

Palace

Here are armchairs in which no one has ever sat,
here are sofas where no one relaxed;
at this desk no one dealt with affairs of state,
handled the miniature obelisk of malachite,
or kept papers in the decorative box.
This magnificent canopy never hung
the anchoring weight of its tassels above
the eyes of anyone
gazing up at its chartreuse and lilac surf;
this is Rome, and Greece, and Paris, arranged
in a whimsical, capricious blend of motifs;
semicircular niches running in a chain;
passages, galleries, columns, and suites;
this is Brenna—molded, patterned, and carpeted
in emerald, violet, whiter than chalk—
squeezing Cameron's beginning out of sight;
Voronikhin continued Brenna's unfinished work
—it's too much.
                    The capacity of the soul,
so it seems, is too small to endure all this.
As the darkness falls
and footsteps die out, objects' gazes fix
on each other: vases, mirrors, candlesticks.
Over here, in the corner, cloudlike, a plaster god;
there, at home on its table, a lamp has trod
on a pattern traced out entirely in gold
and looks irremovable, as if joined by a weld.
Everything has a particular property—a gleam
or a mist, an allusion to its volume and length.

It's not objects I love, but their link
with the world we live in, into which they come.
If we ever were able to figure out
their patterns, patterns we don't yet understand,
which are powerful, since our eyes are caught
—perhaps we'd be happier after that,
closer to a secret that darkness has screened.

These are halls for phantoms to haunt; this can
almost be called an Italian villa; a paradise
lost, flooded by rain,
covered with snow, so that no one ever walks in
without whispering to his remaining life, "Goodbye!"
This Elysium was made by man with the goal
of betraying confusion in our gaze
as we pass through the rooms like geese, in single file;
in this bedroom, none has lain on this gauzy pink haze.
But the masters of this heaven on earth,
of chandeliers like the sun, of chalices full of stars,
really lived lower—in the right-hand wing, as I've heard.
Gilded objects, or waxed—all a material mirage!
And yet once, amid these marble dreams, I was kissed,
surreptitiously, on the run; we strayed
through these halls till we'd missed
the prescribed path. When I die, my last wish
will be finding that crossing, that very square of parquet.

This wonder on a backdrop of January snow;
Aphrodite, Eros, sculpted clusters of grapes;

the evident swoon that the matted eyeballs show;
a mélange of every flowering, bounty, and age;
and beyond plate-glass windows, the whirl of flakes;
these white muses who went on such a long walk
that a snowstorm covered up the road home;
this dry-as-a-rash, icy milk;
the chill-blue protection that glass becomes . . .
Here there's as much daring and risk, here I find
as much longing and craziness (whichever you prefer),
as in life, which waits, rubbing its temples outside,
whether I do remember and miss her
who has vanished . . .

                  No, too much done, too many years;
I forgot, and let go my hand. I forgot,
and—well, isn't the snow out the window more sparse?
And besides, no one ever sat in these chairs
or kept any papers in that box.

Memoirs

N.V., my girlfriend then, who laughed nonstop
in high school (an S.R., she died in '20),
was with me there; we'd gone out for a walk,
as I recall, through Petrograd in springtime

—this was in '17—and met K.M.
running off to his tutoring; I imagine
we liked him because he was so poor and seemed
grownup (in Taganrog he died by hanging);

and Nadya T. was waiting at the gate
on Kovensky Prospekt near Chiniselli
Circus, where all that year a crowd would meet
for rallies (a Trotskyite, she perished);

at the time, she and Kolya U. were close;
as he liked singing more than politicians
(he, wounded in Crimea in the throat,
went to Paris and died in the Resistance),

he said we should skip the rally and stroll
to his place, where what must have been the highest
window anywhere looked out on the canal;
his sister (who later was to die of typhus)

recited some Akhmatova by heart,
and Borya K., so funny that we almost
collapsed, betrayed a mournful glance (he'd starve
in the blockade), as if of dire foreknowledge;

and to this day I recall the fallen sun,
the pearly sheen spread over that drowsy quarter;
I was retrieved by my older brother (gunned
down in '37) toward morning . . .

1980 – 1987

In one of our darkest, most ghastly,
smog-saturated gardens, among
the trees' mutilated, distressing,
and beautiful rows of trunks,
by a river that looks like an awkward
old invalid lying on his side
(it's called the Yekateringofka,
which barely fits into the line),
not far from the factories' spinning
and weaving and cotton-mill soul,
near the trolley-wired back street winding
behind plants where trucks come and go,
in cloudy, or just smoky, weather,
in the snow of winter's last days,
we settled our coming together
for some inconceivable date.

You made it a promise. Remember.
I fear, though, that there, too, from the start,
one way or another, we'll be spending
half of our lifetime apart,
while this textile mill's in operation
three shifts, all around the clock,
darkening the tiniest spaces
in joining its threads and knots.

Dream

Under the camp tent I lay, listless,
hearing the faraway battle noise outside Troy;
and yet all day the sea's soft boom and foam-white whispers
echoed in my head: "Why so uselessly annoyed?"

Bunches of tiny purple flowers bloomed beside me;
I didn't know their name. Lizards scurried between
    the rocks, their ornamental mail brushed shiny;
and armored beetles, like carnelian scarabs, gleamed.

Appearing like a cloudlet from the sea, my mother
sat beside me, trying with her cool hand to lull
my pain and grief, as if my will might then recover.
    The mist around her glowed like strands of pearl.

Swords ring for nothing now: I've quit fighting any battles;
no friend or flatterer can change my mind on this.
    My face, averted from their prattle,
with sullen shadows will abruptly be eclipsed.

The sand is printed with the rough keel of the trireme.
How happy I would be to leave here on that ship!
though I'm also happy when left alone entirely:
    earth's not an easy place to live.

I must have gone to sleep; I slept—for just a moment,
or for an age?—I grabbed the phone, and through it came
a crackling, scratching, rustling, hissing—and then someone
    cried out, "Patroclus is slain!"

Slain when? What for? But there's no life without Patroclus!
Sorry, I wasn't quite awake; now, what was that?
The world careened. My cheek was wet; I'd hardly noticed . . .
    and then something inside collapsed.

The rustle of trees—what's more sweeping or capacious?
Only the sea's coiling wash at the road's margin.
It's certain that the world's evil never decreases
in quantity, that its percentage, a large one,

exact and eternal, remains—or else something
would burst, violating a principle and cracking
the axis. But treetops and waves are past numbering,
and that is a mercy and great source of gladness.

Or do you think Genius, which the power of nature,
pleased with itself, placed in some long-gone era,
had to live its life a shameful, vulgar creature,
while you were born late—a fortunate error?

Joy won't disappear from this world, nor will evil.
We die; what remains after us is the balance.
If only, through the wormwood and clay, through the gravel,
we could go down to where waves shatter the silence.

Out of the various deaths, he was allowed to choose.
It was a favor, for which he gave his thanks to Caesar.
Death could be a dagger. It could be a noose.
He thought about it. Death, to kill the time, would whisper
superfluous suggestions, impatient at his side:
"Just slit your wrists, or drown, or jump from the rooftop . . ."
Opening a cupboard, he thought of cyanide:
not too bad, but maybe not the best solution.

The Greeks' first love was life, but Rome loved dying more.
Death with dignity: on this point Romans were pedantic.
The Greeks idealized peace, Romans the art of war.
The breath of Greeks drew music from their flutes and panpipes.
The Greeks loved living, sculpting torsos like the clouds
of winter, volumes where deep shadows would lie hiding.
Handing a slave his cloak, he had the light put out.
Greeks loved divining with hot wax; the Romans, dying.

And if you sleep, and if the sheets are clean,
and if you lie beneath a good fresh blanket,
and if you sleep, and if, when you recline,
you are your own boss in the silent blackness,
and if it's what they call a tender night,
and if you sleep, and if you've locked the entry
with your own key, and strangers' speech is not
within your hearing, and silence isn't tempted
by some night music's promised happiness,
and no one pulls the blanket off with shouting,
and if you sleep, and if your cheek is pressed
against the starch-bruised linen, and your drowsy
temple rests heavy on a starchy crease
dried thus beneath an iron or in the sunlight,
and if the fingers' small white herd can graze
trustfully on the bedsheet's outspread country,
and your warm shoulder isn't abruptly jarred,
and barking and loud cries don't pay a visit,
and if you sleep, would you still ask for more?
And is there something more? For us, there isn't.

under the murmur of the waves . . .

—KONSTANTIN BATYUSHKOV

Which poet was the first to bring the sea to us,
punctuating his lines with spray from foggy beaches?
I see a certain curly-headed schoolboy pause
from his eye-opening reading of that poet's riches,
having acquired a love for the rough shores of lands
far to the south; for shores of sailcloth, wet and stretching,
    of stone Olympians
and rays of solar fire—far from his darker section.

. . . Pitch-dark and icy, an expanse of straw-strewn snow
with pine sleighs squealing through interminable shadows . . .
I was dreaming of dancers dancing in an O
    on flower-studded meadows,
and of shores where Aeolus whispers all his words,
    where every cloud-cast image
slants to the sea, with one hand clutching coastal skirts
and one dipped in the curling foam where breakers finish.

Their rhythmics coincide, just as the noise of surf
prompts order in us with its pauses and its singing.
    Whose sorrow was the worse?
Both breathed a heady air; the two can't be distinguished;
inhaling bliss, and spring, and then a bitter scent,
the younger growing stronger, and the older choking
    as if a Borgia's hand
had poisoned his last drink—his eyes would never open.

This captivating sound, this riddling motif,
is with us, though: a flute that woke a century later.

There's endless eloquence in him who praises life
—a homeless praise, behind which tragedy is waiting.
Speak, sleepless one! and deal an unexpected blow
with a blue wave's hot sting on my forgetful temple;
     entice me like the snow-
enshrouded, long-beloved phantom you resemble.

The ancient obol's only button-size,
the sort of change the ferryman's collection
was full of. Though his job, I realize,
was easy, it was bitter, too, no question.

Time has rubbed off the least unevenness,
as ranks of waves smooth pebbles with their grinding.
The exhibition constantly impressed
me with its bronzed and flat-nosed faces pining.

All of them dead. Death wiped them from the earth.
And Phaedra's bitter cries conclude the drama.
So where'd they leave their wealth? The oarsman's purse.
The handful left is maybe two, three drachmae.

Sleep, sleep . . . while you sleep, I'll be here at my desk
reading or writing—and your dream will be a sweet one:
a mass of shadows rising like a flight of steps
that one ray, shooting from its lovely folds, throws light on.

Sleep, sleep . . . don't be afraid to sleep when at your side
you find this friend at work in night's powdery darkness.
All I manage to read through, every word I write,
at this hour is overlaid with gilding at its margins.

I'll throw the shawl with the long fringe over the lamp,
so that if in sleep you look through your half-closed lashes,
there will be this fine woolen line laid over them,
and through the double screen there'll be no chance of passing.

But, surfacing from sleep, only to plunge back in,
you manage to perceive in this deceitful moment
the real that outbewitches dreams, the lamplight sheen
on rolled-up sleeves and the oddly agile shadows looming.

Sleep, sleep . . . while you're asleep for an hour and a half
life leaves you behind; but you shouldn't be afraid of
this laggard interval: you can hear the pen's light scratch,
the rocking blinds, and the raspy breathing of the pages.

The Rooster

Rooster, you monster with a blood-red crest, a jagged,
spongy comb cocked to one side: even in your looks,
your undeniably feral, ancient face, an angered
current runs, as if your eyes might give off sparks.

Oh, how you stamp your feet in place, you weather-beaten,
sinewy, tense animal like an idol in polychrome!
You're warlike, rumpled from battle with a fellow creature,
dirt-spattered, as if you were soothing a burn with loam.

Here you strutted, here you hit the dust all over
again, apparently smeared with clotted blood.
Could there be anyone so pious that he's never
once in his life repudiated life and love?

Wild-eyed, high-strung, hoarse, and out-of-tune screamer,
how sweet it is, as each new morning comes, for us
to start again. How bitter, too: don't you remember
the tears—not our weak ones, but Peter's tears, perhaps?

Rain

Rain I remember; I remember how we
slept under sounds of rain. The glory
of heaven, unfortunately, won't contain
what we have everywhere in spring: the rain.

I can remember how it lashed our windows,
and what a happy dream my sleep would kindle;
how deeply I would sleep—and on my arm
you dozed, light as a sparrow in the dark.

And how it ran and splashed along the gutter;
how beautifully, lightly, we lived together!
Laughter-loving rain, sobbing out in gulps
—the Great Flood didn't scare us with its gulf.

So who's to blame, that sterner times have fallen?
I still recall rain, spring rain in the poplar
and maple, sticky rains that briefly fix
a gilded pattern and, for us, a bliss.

Rain, blessed rain; hell, unfortunately,
will not have rain—wherever we're fated
to go at death, we will find winter, these
and all sounds canceled, stilled by total peace,

covered forever in blank snow, in burning.
I remember rain, its coloratura,
high, million-stringed, incessant, moist,
long-suffering and magnanimous.

But you, unfortunately, are neither cold nor hot.
Oh, would that you were cold, or that you could be hot!
Should we ask John the Evangelist for exegesis?
Should I blaze red like coal? Your trumpeter's high note
—should I hit that, half hearing sickly moans and shouts?
Or turn as sternly blue as the straw-muffled ice is?

But I'm not cold. I see your thistle wink at me;
there, by the roadside, its violet-blue eye nodded:
now my iciness will thaw, my sweaty anger dry,
my angry heat cool off. I stand alone, doubt-haunted
(enough of shouts—maybe what's needed is a sigh),
and all-encompassing pity comes unprompted.
Your world of sorrow, though, is good? or bad? To be
a man in it is harder than to be its prophet.

Just think: if there were still centaurs and sirens,
     besides the women and the men,
the ugly scenes that followed would be agonizing.
We'd witness a vast increase in the lack of sense,
in reasons to be jealous and in grounds for anger.
    Things would get terribly enmeshed,
since neighing and strange melodies could then no longer
be distinguished from intelligible speech.

And singing to us from a branch there'd be a monster;
and then a horse would stamp his foot; and somehow good
and evil would rise up to an entirely other
level from what we live with, and a feather would
spin round . . . How could we be so thoroughly disparaged,
    bringing on ourselves such shame?
Take Ulysses, for example; that's how he carried
on *his* life—how simple things have gotten since that time!

Michelangelo

The creator of the Vatican said it the best:
"If our life is so dear to us, death will be, too—as,
after all, it's the same sculptor's work . . ." Winds that raced
off the river are pimpling the air with gooseflesh
and disheveling the bushes . . . I dreamed we were brought
to a studio, where we saw a startling sculpture;
but another, no worse, sits wrapped up, since it's not
ready yet . . . The particular texture, the grainy luster
of a morning in April were given, perhaps,
so we'd trust the old master in all that's to come later.
The low helmet, the stance—ah, what power it has . . .
Then the ending's no worse than the start of the matter.

Before the War: Recollections

There they sit backstage, the dressing room door open;
they're dressed in khaki shirts or wearing suits.
These are bosses. And this is a dream, probably an omen.
They're having beers together: the actors, too.

Through the blinds I can just see the stage over plywood boxes,
beyond the fabulous curtain's folds.
There, onstage, the plague in Florence, actors' tunic costumes
—and here, the beery, everyday world.

There, onstage, a wisp of smoke, a lavish feast, declamation . . .
From there, after they have suffered and died,
they run off backstage, where Central Planning and Aviation
sit with the youths in this plague-stricken crowd.

Friend, what is this? Doesn't history turn out fiery?
I, coincidental with that fateful time,
had, from childhood on, the feeling that this phantasmagory
of ruination was kin to me, was mine.

Now a sweaty actress takes her paper cap off, jingling
its bells, and says, "It sure is warm out here!"
That's the dream I'm dreaming. Did a brief shadow linger
over them, a shadow of what was near?

"Oh, Ivan Lukyanich, why am I an actress? Why not a flier?"
Her cheap cloth braid has fallen to one side.
And the disinfectant smoke drifts downward offstage, hiding
street life in veils and eating at the eyes.

Bottles fill the table. And the lighting is a glorious crimson.
I've been forbidden to watch this outdoor scene.
All of it is ending: dreams, the film, flirting, and refreshment.
And life. Life, too, has almost reached the end.

While someone sleeps, slumped over his elbows at
the table, sleeping seeming then his lifelong object,
how strange he is, how quiet, his world couplings cut;
how unremembering, unknowing, purely thoughtless.

While someone sleeps, the dream he has is everything
and shows across his features as a hazy presence,
read like a shadow or momentary print
of all that's strange in dream, or that a dream unsettles.

And joy is evident, as on a summer wall
we see the swirling shadow of an oak or maple.
For him, though, in that hidden land, what's visible?
To what is he, beyond us in his sleep, so wakeful?

As long as someone sleeps and there's no sudden slip,
frightening him to death, of his elbow into nothing,
his blind faith here, where good and evil both are mixed,
should even influence the seething world's disruptions.

Glitter, glitter, tumbler under sleeping hands!
And, pile of paper at the table's edge, be brilliant.
As long as someone sleeps, a sympathetic trance
of peace spreads out around him like liquid spilling.

His certainty he'll wake to find the world the same
—where did he get it? We, though, tiptoe in our slippers
through our apartmented confinement past his dream
and gaze, perhaps with jealousy, at this sleeper.

The Hedgerow

May you, a living fence of interwoven branches,
    sidle and wreathe
like smoke, concealing a vision that enchants us,
the vision of life not ours; may you bloom and greet
the air with bursts of new shoots. I like your chaotic,
    unseasoned running in place;
whoever set these bushes in a row cannot have
passed away, though he stirs only on summer days
when, like today, the restless leaves will chafe and whisper.
    No, he is indeed
alive, as you are; I'll stand on the very tips of
my toes, like you . . . oh, what a misty, incredible dream!

We always visit rooms belonging to other people
with much embarrassment; we love their coziness,
a living fence . . . we look, then look away, hopeful
that maybe the wind will bend a twig for us,
    and we will glimpse the lives of others:
    nursing a child, petting a dog.
I walk up as close as I can to the thick lather
of this continuous strip of green, this swirling wall.

It's like the sea whipped by the forces of a tempest,
water more fleeced than sheepskin as it boils and churns
    with a disconsolate impulse,
another living fence, a crashing, convulsive surf.
We didn't swim in the sea in those days, we merely
    walked up, hearts racing, to the edge.
Deliver us from evil, from terror and the fury
of dust; against misfortune be a living defense.

When they're set down as if in soil and cultivated,
    lines written look reliable.
Dreams are mixed up in them; their words aren't unrelated.
Night breathes; it prickles and refuses to stand still.

In the pale gullets of flowers, on twigs and branches,
    a cold sweat starts to shake.
And so, in peace on a marble bas-relief, meanders
a procession of some unremembered royal race.
Briers, fibers, gossamer collect and mingle . . .
We, too, keep moving and are overgrown. What with?
    Stings, consolations, wrinkles.
This hedge, this living fence, is witness that we live.

Chinese names are always full of *q* and *z*.
I can't pronounce Ziao Zie and stumble over naming
Zui Zinqun. However, it isn't hard to read
the shadows on their faces; one could scarcely blame them:

people, extracted skillfully, like crickets, by
the world's most unbelievably observant masters,
are caught by some simple, inoffensive phrase. Sharp eyes
won't fail to note the sidelong glance behind one's glasses.

But what dropped from a raincoat ten years back will serve:
some slips of paper or of tongues that had been wagging.
Beidaihe's beaches are really yellow, so we've heard;
but who believes it, after all that weeding out and digging?

Ziao Zie? Don't get upset, I just imagined you.
Live in these stanzas with Zinqun (also fictitious),
who's doffed the paper cap that stalwartly made it through.
Let's poke our heads into this gap between two bushes:

how brilliantly blue! But Yellow is the name.
That bothers you? Don't waste your puerile attacks on
a reckless language. And isn't everywhere the same?
Our own sea, for example, we call the Black one.

85

Tragedy's easy: once onstage, men wreck or slaughter,
then expiate the murk with enlightenment and tears.
But I fear dramas, Aeschylus. From every quarter
they close in, clasp, and tighten in a vine-like squeeze.
Exitless, repeated dreams, shameless misfortunes,
the deathless Latin of prescription drugs; and then
the loaded moving vans, departures, and divorces . . .
A neighbor looks away—the wit, the harlequin.

In the yard an old man and a sick child are strolling
beside the rustling honeysuckle that a breeze has stirred.
Would you prefer the man to be a drunk or lowlife?
You can't add up all pain or put all wrongs in words.
I'm sure that, even now, there wait undreamed-of horrors.
Beneath your window blinds the sun asserts its rays;
still sleeping? Isn't it for you that next door's quarrels
have paid with their loud banging and their nighttime cries?

Cypress

For this, as well, I love black cypress; and I love
it also for this, as well: that is, for blackness,
for being darkest of all things here. One drooping tuft
hangs, peering from its great height, abandoned, feckless.

I love black cypress for this, as well: that it combs back
its stiff and wiry locks, the needles of the cypress;
for this: that on recalling a cypress chest, I catch
the scent of sleepless poems broken into triptychs.

Those sheets of paper in the stuffy, resinous air,
All through life to fight insomnia and suffocation.
What does the cypress see? A ship on water where
the great wave spires in foamy curls, where wave crests glisten.

We're destined for eternity in this life on earth,
as though in one life ten could be accommodated.
But the endless ends; no matter how familiar
it is, sometimes it lets the night outweigh it.

I love black cypress for this, as well: that, having carved
out creaking stretchers from the wood, people bring them
to bear the sleeping ones back to the ship through the dark,
and black earth burns the occiput as if dreams linger.

Farewell! may you wake in another land, mysterious,
where drought and dust never assault the cypress needles.
For this, as well, I love black cypress: that the best
of obelisks to raise over the dead is a cypress seedling.

Mozart's skull, from between two columns of the news,
calmly eyed us, and we stared back at it in horror.
Why had it been dug up? Its slots, its socket-eyes'
sad gape—was that a dream, or something more straightforward?

Look! Through this turret, through this casing of the skull,
this battered cranial box marred with uneven edges,
music radiates unearthly light: the trill
of a bird's long, clear-throated, eighth-note-filled cadenzas.

I cannot bring myself to love man; sadness clings
like rich soil, unshakable from my thoughts. I pity
mankind and its humanity, since nothing brings
deliverance for man's brow or counts the wrongs committed.

March! into a quicklimed pit, Kolyma's murk, a sack,
the ice, forgetting *Figaro* and all bravado.
A touch of modesty—this lesson brings it back:
the finest stowed third-class and incommunicado.

Hush . . . music's playing. Where? In gardens. And where else?
In exile. In a room. Or tavern. Someone fiddles,
and grief is borne on shoulders frailer than a child's
through Viennese parks, through Siberia's bed of needles.

It so happens you're not yet asleep;
every pin dropped still registers clearly.
But you've let down your guard and let slip
reason's golden lucidity; swirling
in salubrious dream state, you're rapt,
dissolving more deeply and deeply
to peace, when there's a terror-like stab
fiercer than electricity's needles.

Then, as if you'd been struck, you collapse
into shivers—what humiliation.
Did an angel with a trumpet fly past?
Is it better, though, not to be making
guesses? But have you seen how, asleep
on his mat, a dog suddenly twitches?
Ripples trouble the water; the leaves
and boughs fret in a stand of birches.

You're from there: that same family, dark,
crude, numberless, and thrashing;
and, however you try standing apart
from those clammy, sweat-covered masses,
you will nevertheless have to endure,
in the end, their embracing and twining,
while the sky holds a shivering star,
begotten in as dark a beginning.

Domitian, the last cruel and savage emperor,
has been killed off. Now once again they're endorsing
honor and good conscience! Historians will preserve
the list of wrongful deaths and wounds, a painful story.

What pattern is behind blind history? I'm afraid
that it's always a blizzard and a lull. You're living,
soaking up the sun, but don't blame magic or fate
for sending those who sailed before you into oblivion.

You won't turn into fate; you won't turn into gods,
nor augur with birds' entrails. A willful wind may rumple
the sheets, suddenly rip them back and throw them off,
before it starts to creep, mouselike, down into the tunnels

of a Dalmatian mine . . . Any Roman could have said
the same; and we can nod to him with understanding.
Not just rough times, but a wolf befell us; now on its side,
it dulls its howl to a wail, then to mere snarls and whining.

And now it's ready to lick our hands like a dog.
But there's a twenty-first rough beast: who can assure us
how that will be? We laughed ourselves to tears when we saw
the tiny, shivering pups that this bitch wolf nurses.

90

There are two marvels, friend:
they're the moral core and starry skies, in Kant's opinion.
Handled like contraband,
they slip into our poems on the quiet, amid death and disunion,
overpowering our fears, yet undiscerned.

It's not insults but guilt
that will sting; in comparison, insults are to be wished for.
When a wave breaks, it spills
crabs, pebbles, and jellyfish, hurried attendants: a picture
that resembles (doesn't it?) someone else.

When the twittering plaint
of a swallow passes above, its mournfulness stirs recollection.
I see trouble's shadow extend
and a cloak that once again someone can't manage to fasten,
as the clasp shies from his trembling hand.

The pavilion of stars:
who built it and broke our hearts with despair? Night has fallen
—so nobody sees this shame of ours.
Now the gossips and poseurs
are aghast at themselves; their consciences make them solemn.

There's a needle-skinned chill.
No forgiveness and no understanding.
Once you've cried, though, you can sleep. Who instilled
our compassion? The same one who made a dark universe
      splendid
with stars brilliant as gilt.

As Catullus wrote, a man's voice deserts him,
his hearing flies, and his sight betrays him
near the one whose speech and bewitching person
at a distance are in every way pleasing.

This longing, this tendency—how well I recall it—
to see all in a distorting, blinding brightness:
this isn't love; it's infatuation, Catullus.
Nets: our own poet even chose the word for a title.

Till our thirty-fifth year we follow the models
of the ancient Greek tadpoles and Roman minnows.
How well I recall! From open hands we take our fodder;
we try out on ourselves a smile's fugitive brilliance.

We hate and love, and every bit of it's painful.
We draw lovely monsters in our mental pictures.
But to live through to actual love! Seeing all, able
automatically to hear, to speak between kisses . . .

You wrote that "ears ring and buzz in their deafness,"
that "over the eyes a nightlike blackness thickens."
But to live through to love! Its exalted freshness
gives food to hearing and new work to vision.

Notes

Acknowledgments

Notes

By leaving, you opted for space
Dzhankoi is an industrial city of about forty thousand inhabitants in the Crimea.

The Adoration of the Magi
An *Adoration of the Magi* by *Hugo van der Goes* hangs in the Hermitage Museum. The *Volkhonka* is one of the oldest streets in Moscow.

No woman that I'd met before
Dostoevsky's "infernal women" do behave this way: Nastasya Filippovna in *The Idiot* throws money in the fire, and Raskolnikov's sister Dunya in *Crime and Punishment* pulls out a revolver.

In the cold of Petropavlovsk, Peter dreams
Petropavlovsk, also known in English as the Fortress of SS. Peter and Paul, is the oldest part of St. Petersburg, built in 1703–10. The *Neva* is Leningrad's major river. The *horseback idol* refers to Falconet's equestrian statue of Peter the Great, known as the "Bronze Horseman" from Pushkin's long poem of that title.

O fame, you have passed us by like the rain, vanished
The *Moika* is one of Leningrad's rivers.

Apollo in the Snow
The statue, a copy of the Apollo Belvedere, stands in the park of the palace at Pavlovsk, one of the former summer residences of the czars.

Folded Wings
Princess Brambilla refers to an 1820 tale by E.T.A. Hoffmann, first translated into Russian in 1844. A stage version by Aleksandr Tairov was for many years in the repertoire of the Kamerny Theater in Moscow.

Man with a Rose
The poem refers to Frans Hals's *Portrait of a Man* in the Hermitage Museum.

As at every doorstep grow rowan and maple
Bartolomeo Francesco *Rastrelli* (1700–71), the preeminent architect of St. Petersburg during the reign of Empress Elizabeth (1741–62), was known for his work in the Baroque style. Karl Ivanovich *Rossi* (1775–1849) was one of the leading architects of the Russian classical style. The togaed statues are the monuments by the sculptor Boris Orlovsky and the architect Vasily Stasov to two heroes of the war of 1812, General Mikhail Kutuzov and Prince Mikhail Barclay de Tolly, which stand in front of the Kazan Cathedral.

Vyritsa
Vyritsa is a village of thirteen thousand inhabitants, located sixty kilometers south of Leningrad.

I loved. I'd wake, not recollecting myself
The novels of the *old Norwegian*, Knut Hamsun (1859–1952), were especially popular in Russia from the turn of the century to the 1920s.

When it's thirteen below, the mind begins preparing
The description of *that passenger* in the sleigh echoes the fifth stanza of Mandelstam's poem "January 1, 1924." This poem marked the onset of a five-year period of poetic inactivity in Mandelstam's life.

No better fate is given than to die in Rome
In a letter of 1837 to Pyotr Pletnyov, Gogol wrote: "There can be no better fate than to die in Rome. Here a man is a good verst closer to God than anywhere else."

Palace

The palace is that of Paul I at Pavlovsk, begun by Charles *Cameron* (1730s–1812), a Scottish architect of the neoclassical style, in 1782–86, and enlarged and remodeled by Vincenzo *Brenna* (1745–1820) in the 1790s. After a fire in 1803, it was redone by the Russian architect Andrei *Voronikhin* (1759–1814).

Memoirs

An *S.R.* was a member of the Social Revolutionary Party, a group outlawed by the Bolsheviks after the October Revolution. The *Chiniselli Circus* no longer exists in Leningrad; it was previously located on the Fontanka River.

In one of our darkest, most ghastly

The *Yekateringofka* is a small river in the southwest part of Leningrad.

Which poet was the first to bring the sea to us

Batyushkov (1787–1855) is the older poet discussed in the poem, and Aleksandr Pushkin (1799–1837) is the younger. The *flute* in the last stanza refers to Osip Mandelstam (1891–1938?).

But you, unfortunately, are neither cold nor hot

The first two lines are a citation from Revelation 3:15.

Before the War: Recollections

The play being presented in the poem is Pushkin's *Feast during the Plague.*

Chinese names are always full of *q* and *z*

Beidaihe is a beach resort near Beijing, a favorite vacation spot for officials.

Cypress

The *sleepless poems* are those of Innokenty Annensky (1856–1909), whose book *The Cypress Chest* is arranged in twenty-five triptychs. Annensky suffered from insomnia.

Mozart's skull, from between two columns of the news
Osip Mandelstam disappeared in a labor camp in *Kolyma*. *The Marriage of Figaro* was a favorite opera of his.

There are two marvels, friend
A discussion of *Kant*'s proofs of the existence of God occurs in the opening chapter of Mikhail Bulgakov's novel *The Master and Margarita*. In the third stanza of the poem, the figure who grasps at the clasp of his cloak is Pontius Pilate, from the second chapter of the same novel.

As Catullus wrote, a man's voice deserts him
The Catullus poem in the first stanza is no. 51, itself a free translation of one of Sappho's. Stanza four begins with the opening phrase of Catullus no. 85, the famous couplet *"Odi et amo."* *Nets* was the first book of poetry by Mikhail Kuzmin (1875–1936).

Acknowledgments

The translators would like to express their thanks to the following individuals: John Malmstad, for first introducing Carol Ueland to the poetry of Aleksandr Kushner; Vassa Shevel, for her assistance to Paul Graves in reaching the first drafts of several of these translations; Joseph Brodsky, for his unfailing support at all times; Jane Bobko, whose care for the word constantly improved our work; the late Rose Raskin, whose knowledge of Russian poetry was exceeded only by her generosity in sharing it; and, finally, Aleksandr Kushner, who spent many hours with us, both in New York and in Leningrad, discussing the interpretation of his poems.

P.G.
C.U.